The Story of Dawlish Warren

Chips Barber

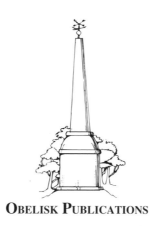

OBELISK PUBLICATIONS

ALSO BY THE AUTHOR:

Dawlish and Dawlish Warren in Colour
Dawlish of Yesteryear • Discovering Devon…Dawlish
The Story of Hallsands • The Story of Dartmoor Prison
Devon's Wild and Wicked Weather • Devon's Amazing Men of God *(with Walter Jacobson)*
Ten Family Bike Rides in Devon
Ten Family Walks on Dartmoor • Six Short Pub Walks on Dartmoor
Short Circular Walks in and around Sidmouth • Walks on and around Woodbury Common
Diary of a Dartmoor Walker • Diary of a Devonshire Walker
The Great Little Dartmoor Book • The Great Little Exeter Book
The Great Little Totnes Book • The Great Little Plymouth Book • The Great Little Chagford Book
Made in Devon • The Dartmoor Quiz Book • Place-Names in Devon • An A to Z of Devon Dialect
Dark & Dastardly Dartmoor • The Ghosts of Exeter • Haunted Pubs in Devon
Ghastly & Ghostly Devon • The Lost City of Exeter – Revisited
Exmouth in Colour • Plymouth in Colour
Beautiful Exeter • Colourful Dartmoor • Colourful Cockington • Topsham in Colour
The South Hams in Colour • Torbay in Colour – Torquay, Paignton, Brixham
Sidmouth Past and Present • Topsham Past and Present • Honiton Past and Present
Seaton & Axmouth • Beer • Branscombe • Colyton & Colyford
Around & About Salcombe • Around & About Teignmouth
Around & About Hope Cove and Thurlestone • Around & About Burgh Island and Bigbury-on-Sea
Around & About Tavistock • Around & About Roborough Down • Around & About Lustleigh
Kingskerswell of Yesteryear *(with John Hand)* • Shaldon & Ringmore
Dawlish and Dawlish Warren • The South Hams • Torquay • Paignton • Brixham
From The Dart to The Start • Dartmouth and Kingswear
Brixham of Yesteryear, Parts I, II and III • Pinhoe of Yesteryear, Parts I and II
Princetown of Yesteryear, Parts I and II • The Teign Valley of Yesteryear, Parts I and II
Widecombe – A Visitor's Guide • Bickleigh – A Visitor's Guide
Newton Ferrers and Noss Mayo • Along The Otter • Along The Tavy • Along The Avon
Railways on and around Dartmoor • Devon's Railways of Yesteryear
Chagford of Yesteryear • Dartmoor of Yesteryear • Exminster of Yesteryear • Dartmouth of Yesteryear
Heavitree of Yesteryear • Sidmouth of Yesteryear • Whipton of Yesteryear
Plymouth Hoe • Tiverton
Walk the East Devon Coast – Lyme Regis to Lympstone
Walk the South Devon Coast – Dawlish Warren to Dartmouth
Walk the South Hams Coast – Dartmouth to Salcombe
Walk the South Hams Coast – Salcombe to Plymouth

OTHER BOOKS ABOUT THIS AREA

Pub Walks in and around the Haldon Hills, *Brian Carter*
Kenton and Starcross of Yesteryear, *Eric Vaughan*
Around the Churches of the Teign Valley, Parts 1 and II, *Walter Jacobson*
Exmouth of Yesteryear, *Kevin Palmer*
Strange Stories from Exmouth, *Tricia Gerrish*
Exmouth to Starcross – An Ancient Ferry, *W H Pascoe*
Exmouth Century Parts 1 and 2, *George Pridmore*

For a full list of our current books, please send SAE to
2 Church Hill, Pinhoe, Exeter, EX4 9ER
or visit our website at <u>www.ObeliskPublications.com</u>

Acknowledgements

Thanks to Mrs Andrews for old pictures and her memories; Mr Norton for page 23; Anthony Westell for his reminiscences. All other pictures taken by or belonging to Chips Barber.

First published in 2001, reprinted in 2002 and 2008 by
Obelisk Publications, 2 Church Hill, Pinhoe, Exeter, Devon
Designed and Typeset by Sally Barber
Printed in Great Britain

© Chips Barber/Obelisk Publications 2001

The Story of Dawlish Warren

There are two contrasting environments at Dawlish Warren: one is the tourist attraction of amusements, pubs, cafés, shops, sprawling holiday camps, car parks and sandy beach; the other is the acres of untamed dunescape and broad estuary inhabited by numerous species of wildlife including an amazing bird population.

In the tourist Warren the amusement arcades are a colourful adornment with kiddies' rides outside each 'fun palace'. The infant Warren 'fun-seeker' can experience the gyrations of a Postman Pat Mobile, complete with black and white cat, or perhaps a really cute, garishly green dinosaur playing a saxophone – a case of whatever turns you on, or around, or up, or down! Beyond the claustrobically low railway tunnel ('the Creep'), where visitors enter the Warren, there are many more rides and 'games of skill' for the holidaymaker to enjoy.

The changing nature of Dawlish Warren's sandspit is a geographer's dream because it's the classic environment for fieldwork studies, an interface or 'battlefield' between land and sea. Many text books about physical geography include a few pages about the Warren, but it is usually presented in a clinical and purely objective way.

Throughout the year students of all shapes, sizes and ages are brought to the Warren to see how Man attempts to keep that age-old enemy, the sea, at bay. For them the Warren is purely an example of a sandspit, a place where the various on-going processes of coastal erosion and deposition can be observed, measured and analysed. But there's far more to the Warren than meets the eye and they would do well to know a bit about its past in order to understand its present and possibly even its future.

Most people who visit the Warren simply do so for leisure and pleasure reasons, perhaps for a game of golf, bird-watching, fishing, a stroll along the beach, or along the path on the crest of the dunes. From the latter it's possible to appreciate not only why the Warren itself is such a wonderful place but also why the Devonshire landscape is so revered. The views, inland over the Haldon Hills, northwards up the estuary, or along the seaboard, from the distant grey limestone bastion of Berry Head to the richly red cliffs of Sandy Bay and beyond, where headland after headland fades into the distance, are stunning.

The Warren's golf course was formed in 1892 by enthusiasts. The first club house was built in 1904 but has changed much since that time, the facilities being upgraded to meet changing demands. One of the keenest golfers, in the club's earliest days, was Colonel Fox, a member of a wealthy Quaker family whose company manufactured Fox's Puttees, worn by troops of the British army during the First World War. Their firm was based in Taunton and it was from there that the Colonel travelled to play a round of golf. He enjoyed the privileged position of being able to catch any train to the Warren, even those that were not scheduled to stop there. The Colonel, as a director of the Great Western Railway and a Gold Pass holder, could request any train to stop at any station without fear of penalty.

After the Second World War another enthusiastic golfer, Colonel Creasy of Exeter, bought the land on which the course is laid out from the Earl of Devon, to enable the club to develop. When he died the land was bequeathed to the Devon Trust for Nature Conservation and now, as a Site of Special Scientific Interest, cannot be developed without permission.

The course is quite a challenge, possibly the best and the worst place to play golf: there are probably no better surroundings to enjoy a round but all sorts of obstacles exist to make it the most cussed of games. Accuracy and straight driving are the operative words here. If you stand on the path that runs along a ridge in the dunes you will be able to witness players 'enjoying' the time-honoured ritual of looking for lost balls.

You will have to consult the *Guinness Book of Records* to discover the longest recorded *bona fide* golf drive but the Warren's 'record' is believed to be a staggering 200 miles! A golfer, out on the links early one morning, at the 18th hole, hit too strong a shot, which arrowed through the window of a Paddington-bound train. Or is this just another golfing tale?

In August 2000 one of my childhood heroes achieved a rarity in golfing circles when the score for his round was less than his age! Former Exeter City FC stalwart Arnold Mitchell, who made a record 495 appearances for the Grecians, carded a 68 when he was 70!

Birdwatchers might see the Warren's most important function as a habitat for the other type of 'birdies'. The estuary is famed for its bird-life and the hide at the back of the Warren is definitely a place to seek if you have an interest in ornothology.

We continue with a potted history lesson. During the English Civil War (1642–1646) there was a Royalist fort on the tip of what was a more expansive area of sand-dune country. According to the *Cambridge History of Devon* the fort had 16 guns but *Memorials of Exmouth* states it had 13! The number is purely academic because the fort was outgunned and surrendered to Colonel Shapcote late in the conflict.

In 1782 a privateer from Flushing fought a sea battle with the English ship the *Defiance*. The Dutch ship, *Zeuce*, was defeated and many of her dead were buried in the sands. Their ghosts have been heard to wail but this just might be the wind whistling through the marram grass! The one local man to die was William Bence, who was buried at Littleham on 14 June.

The Warren is an ever-changing topographical feature, as will be very evident later. As long ago as 1817 some five acres were washed away in a single storm. At this time the sands extended over a much larger area and where the Shutterton Brook met the estuary, in a swampy location, there were salt pans. It's not known exactly when these stopped being productive but they were in business in 1750, when John Bannister was the 'Salt Officer' for Kenton. The place where this brook trickles through the Exe estuary mud at low water, at the back of the Warren, is called 'Salthouse Lake'.

In 1844, when a much bigger 'Warren' extended to some 300 acres, the King of Saxony visited a saltworks which was 'in the heart of the dunes'.

The Warren stretches out for almost one and half miles and its tip is not far from the entrance of Exmouth Docks, a place whose own environs have seen immense change in recent years. The gap between the sandspit and the docks has varied considerably throughout the years, because of the building up, or destruction, of the sandy spit and the changing nature of the course of the Exe as it greets the sea.

It was passed on by word of mouth, from generation to generation, that Anne Lytton (or Litten), who lived in Exmouth from 1715 to 1805, often used to make her way *'to milk the cows grazing'* on the Warren, via a series of 'stepping stones'. Late Victorian 'experts' in such matters believed that either the Bull Hill (now a mudbank) or the Shilley (an area adjacent to Exmouth Docks, now better known as 'The Shelly'), which were then sandhills as high as those of the Warren, may have been where Anne wandered all those years ago. But according to Anne's grandson, Samuel Bricknell, his ancestors vividly recalled that the main channel from the estuary into the sea was beside Langstone Point, so perhaps this seemingly fanciful notion was true after all. There is a cliff here to back up the theory.

In 1816 there was a steep bluff of sand at the Exmouth end of the Warren that was 25 feet high. The gap between the end of the Warren and Exmouth was estimated at being less than 180 yards but the width of the Exe's mouth never remained constant. In 1851 it was 542 yards; in 1938 it was back down to a mere 253 yards; within another six years it was 625 yards.

There was a report in the long-extinct *Woolmer's Gazette* in 1845 that an unknown pioneer flew from the Exmouth side of the estuary to land on the Warren. *"To the amazement of several Exmothians in 1845, at daybreak, a strangely-clad man, was seen to leave the beach, near the sea wall, by a series of motions similar to those of a bird attempting to take off. It was reported that indeed this pioneer did in fact fly over the water, landing safely on the Warren."*

Whilst some men were struggling with the wonders of human flight, more terrestrially-minded folk, like the famous Isambard Kingdom Brunel, were giving their attentions to the building of railways. The first line reached Exeter from London on 1 May 1844 and after that it was developed southwards on to Dawlish, Teignmouth and beyond.

The initial single line of the mid-1840s took a lowland route meeting the Exe Estuary near Powderham's church. Brunel anticipated little problem with this watery encounter. The route was to be along the edge of the river bed but he soon discovered that the estuarine mud was much deeper, in places, than he had expected. He thus built the line on a man-made embankment and there were places, between Powderham and the Warren, where the railway was 100 yards or more out from the 'mainland'. The tidal water was allowed to enter or leave the landward side of the embankment by a series of tunnels. The task of reclaiming this land, not a difficult one, was completed in the 1850s. There are, therefore, people who now live on the former river bed and also holiday camps located on it. This reclaimed land is largely that which lies between the railway line and the road which runs from Cockwood to Dawlish Warren.

The Warren marked the point where the railway left the estuary to follow the red sea-cliffs towards Dawlish. To do so it cut through Langstone Point to turn it, almost as if by magic, into Langstone Rock, Devon's mini-Ayers Rock. The tiny café, which is now at its base is aptly called the Red Rock Café. This distinct outcrop, now virtually cut into two, affords fine views from its summit. Although it is also a favoured point for rail enthusiasts to take pictures of passing trains, it remains a potentially dangerous vantage point, as warning signs point out. Beneath Langstone Rock there are some impressive caves. In the past it was often used as a refuge during

thunderstorms but a wary eye had to be kept, because the quick-rising tide was always liable to catch people out.

When the railway first operated trains did not stop at the Warren. There seemed little reason to put a 'halt' in the middle of an unpopulated sandy wasteland.

Perhaps having seen Brunel's achievements, an ambitious scheme was considered by the Earl of Devon in 1862. His cunning plan, for which he gained permission from the Board of Trade, was to build an embankment from Warren Point along the estuary to Starcross, thereby enclosing an extensive area for an oyster farm. To facilitate the transport of the 'harvested' oysters he intended to construct a pier, which would be linked to a siding off the passing South Devon Railway. He believed that the soft blue clay lining the estuary bed would be ideal for an oyster farm. But his lordship must have got cold – or perhaps muddy – feet, because the plan gave way to a more modest venture which was to last just two years.

In 1867 the sheltered Greenland Lake, a former tidal inlet between the Inner and Outer Warren, became the chosen spot of the Exe Bight Oyster Fishing and Pier Company, which laid down almost 30,000 oysters in beds. This enterprise also lasted just two years, coming to an abrupt end in 1869, when a storm ripped through the Warren and the displaced sands were dumped on top of the oysters.

When the tide was out, the Bight, at the back of the Warren, took on the appearance of a muddy hollow, with sand flats appearing and tiny silver streamlets running through at low water. It was here that those strange creatures of the creek, the cockle women, were to be seen bent at their work for hours at a time. These ladies stayed at their workaday task until the sea sent in its tide to halt their activities. This is Jane Lane, subject of a number of picture postcards of that era. She would, no doubt, have been amazed if she knew how 'famous' she was to become, many years later, as a result of her somewhat moist and muddy 'modelling career'.

Up to the 1890s the Warren saw but a few visitors of the human variety. Those who came, mainly from Exeter, often walked some three to four miles from the railway station at Starcross. It was usually young and energetic men who made the effort required to enjoy the Warren's exciting environment where the wind and waves always held sway.

In 1905 the Great Western Railway eventually saw the potential of this 'wasteland' and built the first platforms. Warren Halt became a popular venue, particularly for people from Exeter. The platforms were lengthened, out of necessity, in 1907 and the facilities were improved. The number of visitors continued to increase and in 1912 a new station opened, some 400 yards away, to be called 'Dawlish Warren', the first time we hear of this place-name, 'christened' by the GWR.

The Warren had its own special aromas and 'old stagers' recalled the pleasure from the odours of sea and tar *"mingled with the honey and almond of the heather and the gorse."* With their tea some visitors would enjoy a meal of cockles that had been gathered in the Bight and boiled over a wood fire, made from driftwood. *"The scent was sensational – the bees droned, the larks sang, the sun was always shining ..."*

Those guide book writers of yesteryear, whose job it was to travel around the county, paid scant attention to the Warren. It was simply tagged on as an afterthought when portraying the established delights of neighbouring Dawlish. In 1907 Mr Harper was one of the few to register his observations. *"Until quite recently the Warren has remained the haunt of the wild-fowler and the naturalist, but now the red roofs of bungalows*

are beginning to plentifully dot the wastes; and to play at Robinson Crusoe, with twentieth-century embellishments and more or less luxurious fringes, has become a favourite pastime on this once solitary haunt of the heron, the wild duck and the sea-mew [gulls]."

And so we hear mention, for the first time, of the colony of bungalows once found at the Exmouth end of the Warren spit. This was then often known as 'Exmouth Warren' because it was closer to Exmouth than Dawlish. It's believed that the first of the bungalows was built in 1899 and it wasn't long before many others followed in its wake.

Field's Shanty had a turret and a circle of protecting conifers. According to local gossip, its owner, Mr Field, left the Warren 'under a cloud', apparently in order to avoid hordes of debtors.

Some of these summer dwellings were quite grand and one even had a tennis court.

Mr Templeman of Exeter was a pioneer settler who enjoyed the sea and the invigorating salt air. His first bungalow, which he bought in 1900, was called 'La Casetta' (shown opposite). After a few years he had to disassemble it and move it to a safer site as the sea had encroached to within yards. After several years without problems the sea again threatened; in 1914 the bungalow was

moved into the heart of the well-established 'village' of strange-looking, summer-only dwellings located in the centre of the dunes. La Casetta was resited beside a building called 'The Tea House'. But names can sometimes be deceptive, because cups of tea were not served here! This was the Outer Warren's shop, a meeting place where people came to collect or buy their provisions, including tea, and as such was a social place where much dune gossip was exchanged. The life-essential commodities obtained or collected included bread and milk, paraffin and post. All of these came by ferry from Exmouth or along from Starcross. There were many ferrymen prepared to make the crossing of this perilous estuary mouth. Kingly tolls were extracted from short-term guests, 'regulars' being charged more 'realistic' dues.

The Outer Warren families were largely dependent on the ferrymen who operated a fetching and carrying service between Exmouth Pier and the sand-spit. These included, in the early decades of the twentieth century, Mr Vicary, deaf Jan White, Bill Luscombe ('King of the Boatmen') and Bill Hocking, who was assisted by his son, Tom. These adaptable characters supplemented their incomes by doing all sorts of extra little jobs; Bill Hocking had the unenviable task of cleaning out the sewage pits at The Cabin.

This was written in 1926 for a book called *Unknown Devon: "A longshoreman will put you across on Dawlish Warren and a couple of miles along soft sand will bring you to the farther mainland. I have often tramped that two miles, and the yielding desert does not make harder going. I always think that a system of camel transport ought to be instituted along the Warren, it is so obviously the place for camels; their silhouetted forms, moving statelily along the ridge of the sand hillocks, would give a piquantly Oriental look to the scene ..."*

Since 1984 a water taxi has operated between Exmouth Docks and the seaward end of the Warren. In the past there was a ferry service to remove the need of a long inland detour. But things were not always rosy for wayfarers. And not always is the weather in Devon as fair as the guide books and the locals might like to claim! In 1817 the facilities for awaiting the ferry drew this report from the local press: *"A very respectable correspondent at Exmouth expresses his surprise that no shed or other shelter has ever been erected on the shore of the ferry over to The Warren, to protect passengers who have to await the arrival of the ferry boat in that exposed situation – often valetudiarious [sic], chilling after a warm walk in the cold sea breeze and not infrequently exposed to pelting showers. It is well known that some serious colds have been caught there under such circumstances and perhaps some fatal ones."*

La Casetta rose high above many of the other rooftops. Despite its substantial structure its days were numbered and it fell victim to the fickle whims of the sea. But Mr Templeman was not the sort of man to let the marram grass grow beneath his feet, and he took a fancy to another bungalow, this time one called 'Numerella', which had been built in 1909. This was to serve him well until the mid-winter of 1937, when a series of storms, combined with high tides, started removing almost all in their wake. The Exeter man was fortunate because he salvaged his building and possessions just a day ahead of when they would have been washed away.

Another close encounter of the maritime type occurred in the deep winter of 1925 when a well-known local citizen had taken a shine to one of the other bungalows on the Outer Warren. He had instructed his solicitor 'to complete' on the first Friday in January and decided to go down to the Warren one last time on Thursday, New Year's Eve, to see the object of his desire. When he got there he discovered the bungalow that he was about to buy, the very next day, had been washed away that morning. The only thing that remained was the sand on which it formerly stood.

There is an ever-diminishing band of folk who can recall, with any accurate detail, these strange structures of the Outer Warren. Joan Andrews (née Fulford) is one of them, a lady who helped me illustrate what the Outer Warren looked like all those years ago by lending many of the old pictures included here and by sharing her memories with me.

She has a unique claim to fame because, she believes, she is the only baby to be born on the Outer Warren. She is quick to add, *"But not the only one conceived there!"* I wonder if any of them were named 'Sandy' or 'Warren'!

Joan's christening took place in 1916 at the lovely church of St Mary's, at nearby Cofton; although she could not remember the occasion herself, she knew that the family hired one of the Exmouth ferry boatmen to convey them from their Warren home up the estuary and into Cockwood Harbour. From here they made their way on foot the short distance inland to the church.

Mrs Andrews' father was Sidney Fulford, who had fallen in love with the wide open expanses of the Warren in the late 1890s. He built a small, humble abode called 'The Look-Out', quite possibly the first substantial structure on the highest sandy bluff at the far end of the spit. Sidney was a master builder and saw that here

there was scope for a much grander building. He envisaged a small castle with leaded windows, oak panelling and even a coat of arms! This he achieved with his new home that he ingeniously called St Eame. This was not named after any favourite patron saint but his brothers and sisters: he took the first letter of his and their Christian names. Thus **S**idney, **T**homas, **E**llen, **A**nnie, **M**innie and **E**thel contrived to give him an unusual name for his sandy dwelling. Also known as St Eame's Burrow, it entertained a variety of guests; a note in the visitors' book from Jacky White summed up what the Warren was all about. *"Enjoyed ourselves a treat. I have visited many parts of the world but it is difficult to find a spot where freedom and liberty obtains more than here."*

Under the heading 'The Gale', this is part of a report from the *Gazette* which appeared Monday, 11 December 1911, when Sidney's house faced immense difficulties.

"The gale of Saturday night and Sunday morning, when the eighty miles an hour wind drove huge waves on to the Dawlish Warren, carried on the work of destruction which was begun on the previous Thursday. The sea then cut away, in many places, the banks of sand and wiregrass which formed a natural protection for the bungalows, and made channels through from the seashore to the little bay which, at high tide, divides the popular side of the Warren from the golf course. 'The Rest', belonging to Mr Aspinall, and a bungalow belonging to Mr S. Fulford, of Exeter, were then within a yard or two of the edge of the bank, and fears were expressed that a repetition of the high seas would prove disastrous to them.

Unfortunately for the owners named, the gale of Saturday night washed away the remaining sand bank in front of the bungalows, and while 'The Rest' is now in a slight hollow with its seaward foundations exposed and banks of sand on each side, Mr Fulford's bungalow is practically done for. It was built about eight years ago, thirty yards from the edge of the sand bank, which was about twenty feet above the seashore. The bank has been gradually washed away and a neat little look-out tower, which was a short distance to the westward of the bungalow, disappeared in the gales last March ...

Last Thursday a portion of the garden was washed away, and on Sunday morning the ground underneath the front room disappeared in the sea, and about six feet of the bungalow is hanging down over the sands below; and is likely to fall. Mr Fulford, who sees no hope in saving the bungalow, has removed the oak panelling and the chimney …

The major portion of the Warren, from the Bathing Office at the end of the path (which structure was also undermined on Sunday, propped up and yesterday removed to a higher piece of ground) to the first bungalow, is now practically flat sands. The channel cut through into the Bight is eighty yards wide, and on Sunday morning the waves rushed through it like a torrent, and several bungalows facing Exmouth had their foundations exposed. The high path made by railway sleepers and boulders near the station is unsafe to walk on. On each side of it are great holes …"

Maurice Drake, an Exeter clockmaker (some sources say glass painter) and author, owned one of the other earliest Warren bungalows, from 1899, and 'took time out' to stay at the Warren throughout at least twelve summers. He was on a committee set up, in December 1911, to discuss ways of saving the Warren from extinction. There was a strong difference of opinion between him and Mr Fulford over the possible placement of groynes on the beach and both men wrote exceedingly long letters, contradicting each other, to the local press. Maurice passed away in 1923. One of his novels, *WO2*, featured a train robbery in a tunnel on the railway between Dawlish and Teignmouth. The opening scene was at Dawlish Warren.

Another committee member was Mr Alford, who stated that the defence of the Warren was not just for the 'boathouse owners' and added that it was an attraction to the City of Exeter and the town of Exmouth and that there were public rights of way over it. If nothing was done then it would be to the detriment of the navigation of the Bight and Exmouth Docks would suffer. The debate was long and sometimes very heated.

The Devon Fortress Royal Engineers had been actively engaged, on Saturday afternoons, in the years between 1909 and 1911, in erecting brushwood revetments to hold the sand in check. They had been pleased with their endeavours but must have looked on in dismay as the sea removed much of their work with ease.

Undeterred by his losses and problems Sidney Fulford took a daring and somewhat defiant step by building an even bigger and better home on the dunes, but at a much safer distance from the marauding sea. The new venture was the two-storey one shown here, a splendid building, again with a tennis court.

Sidney had to commute to work in Exeter. The first part of the journey was the wearisome walk to the Warren station. The attire suitable for beach life was not the same as that for working in the city. He partly overcame his 'dress-code' problems by striking a deal with the stationmaster. At the Warren station he would discard his beach-wear and change into more conventional city clothes, which he kept there, leaving his Warren-wear ready for when he arrived back. And so the routine went on working like clockwork most of the time … but when he was 'running late' he would climb aboard the Exeter-bound train in a state of transition, having to throw his sand shoes back on to the platform as the locomotive pulled out of the station!

Whilst Sidney worked his two children enjoyed the freedom and the fresh air. They learnt how to catch fish, gathered driftwood for fuel that crackled loudly as it burnt, and formed an impressive and colourful collection of shells.

All was well with their impressive Warren home until the 1920s, when it met the same fate as its predecessor. This time the family were most fortunate in timing their evacuation. Had they chosen to sit out the storm they would have been washed away with it!

Sidney, although something of a romantic, was also a realist. He went back to the Warren the next day and, although crestfallen at what he saw, managed to salvage what he could. In the short term he made plans to live a more regular existence in Exeter, where he built a home at Taddyforde, high on a bluff above St David's Station.

From the wreck of his Warren home he built a more modest summer hut that was to serve his family and friends for the best part of the next few decades. Some of the finer salvaged items, like the oak panelling and leaded windows, were incorporated into the new Fulford residence in Exeter. I have sat on the chair seen behind Mr Fulford in this 1916 picture, and also held the wonderful barometer, with a miniature pair of oars on its top, which can be seen on the mantelpiece.

Water, the fresh variety, was a problem for almost all the properties. Those whose huts were closest to the station had it piped in but those 'castaways' on the Outer Warren had to collect their own supplies from strategically placed tanks or roof-top butts; water was a precious commodity and not a drop was wasted.

The 1920s were a decade of surprises and shocks. Despite the upset of those who lost their holiday homes, there were the occasional finds. A mussel yielded what came to be known as the revered 'Warren Pearl': an enormous, button-shaped black pearl that caused much excitement amongst jewellers in Exmouth.

Deck House was an unusual abode because it was built on stilts! It was so named for the simple reason that this raised structure, often only reached after wading through water, had a verandah around it on all sides. A line of nautical flags was attached to one of its neighbouring bungalows, called 'The Stilts'. This was the work of a retired naval sea captain and presented the message, *"Come in and have one if you can read this."*

The Cabin, mentioned earlier, was another Bohemian abode and was owned, after 1926, by an Exeter man called Westell who loved the Warren life, in particular that part which took place on the golf course. Three decades later, after retirement, he became the club secretary. In the 1920s he had been given the perfect excuse for buying this wooden structure with its corrugated iron roof, a living room and three bedrooms (two of which resembled horse boxes). His son, Anthony,

born in January 1926, was found to be suffering from a problem in his digestive system. The doctor had recommended that he should be taken to the South of France to spend time in a climate that would help restore his health. His father opted for the Warren bungalow. The climate must have worked a treat because Anthony wrote to me in his seventieth year, from his home in Toronto, to tell me of his memories of those dune-loving days where the Warren played its part in his recuperation.

The bungalow had been bought from two bachelors who had chosen to decorate the table in the main room for roulette. This was one of many unusual Warren artifacts to be washed away in the winter storms of 1939/40.

It was more or less accepted that everyone who spent time at the Warren was equally at home on or in the water, for there was no getting away from it. Anthony Westell recalled moonlight journeys on the shiny, silvery sea or up the glistening estuary, where his father created an everlasting 'moon-over-water' memory when he rowed them beneath starry skies.

Such unconventional residences attracted some equally unusual, eccentric dune dwellers. There was a lady who flew the white ensign of a Vice-Admiral of the Fleet, contrary to all rules and regulations. This streamed outwards proudly in the breeze. Had the law desired to take her to task her actions would have resulted in a hefty fine. Other Warren residents were curious about this hermit-like lady's reasons for this act but no satisfactory explanation was ever given.

The comedian Tommy Cooper had fond recollections of Dawlish Warren. In 1925, when he was just four years old, he had been brought to Exeter from Wales. His parents, Gertrude and Tommy senior, bought No 3 Fords Road in the St Thomas district of Exeter. As a young boy he assisted his parents in selling ice creams from the window of their home and also travelled 'in the season' to Dawlish Warren, to sell ices to trippers on the beach. His interest in magic was probably cultivated by an aunt in Aylesbeare who bought him his first conjuring set. He used it to entertain and amaze his fellow schoolmates at the Mount Radford School, which

then existed at the bottom of St Leonard's Road in Exeter. Following a glittering career his life was brought to a sudden end in 1984, when he collapsed and died whilst performing in a show with Jimmy Tarbuck. A campaign, spearheaded by Exeter's evening paper the *Express & Echo*, led to this plaque being placed on his former Exeter home.

The Warren has always been an atmospheric place; to stand, in relative safety on some high point, to witness towering waves is an exciting experience. But to be placed in a life-threatening situation, or one where your property is at risk, is an altogether different prospect. Here are some extracts taken from newspaper articles that help to convey what the Warren can be like at times of storm and tempest. The first report is an account given by Mrs Warne of 33 Magdalen Street, Exeter in March 1928. She owned a bungalow called 'Shalet' and had this to say in the *Express & Echo.*

"I was scrubbing the floor, and my son was doing a bit of painting. We were about to leave, when to our horror and dismay we saw that our plight was indeed desperate, for we were surrounded by water. In a vain endeavour to reach our car, which was in the parking place by the restaurant, we tried to wade through the floods. I never, before, had such a terrifying experience, and it all seemed like some awful nightmare. As we went forward so our predicament became worse, and it was not long before we were both waist high in water. Spurred on by the hope of reaching the sanctuary of the mainland I wanted to continue but it was then that my son reminded me that there was a sharp descent of about 13 feet near at hand. His presence of mind undoubtedly saved my life.

Meanwhile the fury of the storm showed no signs of abating, and before long we were compelled to enter a cellar of a neighbouring bungalow. As the creek began to run out we renewed our attempt to wade through the floods, and it was just before eleven o' clock at night that we regained our car. Even that was submerged right up to its wings and we had a hard struggle before starting her."

In the following days there were some abnormally high tides and the water broke through Crispin's Restaurant. This was a family-run business, started in 1906 from a tent, and later became a substantial property where bungalow owners and visitors could also order their provisions.Their 'Refreshment House' was then the only place, on the coast road between Starcross and Dawlish, where it was possible to buy groceries.

Despite the rising waters the Crispin clan made good their escape. The floods poured through the arch beneath the railway bridge at the entrance to the Warren. It was possible to row a boat from Exmouth all the way to the Warren station. Some did it for sheer bravado and, on arriving at the bottom of Mount Pleasant, beached their boat at the bottom of the hill before walking to the top of it to get liquid refreshment at the Mount Pleasant Inn.

One of the major causes of such serious flooding, according to those who lived there, had been the removal of vast quantities of sand used in the building of new houses in the vicinity. It was even believed that much of the beach material was going as far as Newton Abbot. Even whilst the floods were raging, there were carts willing to take risks to continue extracting sand.

Various people lost their holiday homes in this particular flood. Mr Biddlecombe of Pinhoe had recently bought a property and was assured, in his own mind, of its structural stability because in front of it were railway sleepers to a height of nine feet and behind it a ten-foot-high bank of sand. The sea made short shrift of all this and items of his furniture were seen floating in the sea.

A similar fate was suffered by well-known Exeter business man Walter Otton, whose shop in Fore Street was a place of 'pilgrimage' for almost every Exonian handyman in those days before

DIY superstores. His and his brother Reg's Warren bungalow was about the third closest to the railway station. It was a beautiful building, the work of Mr Locke, an eminent architect, and known as the Round House. Beside it a windmill used to pump flood or rain water off the greens of the golf course. Despite its apparent strength, the Round House was carried some fifteen yards across the golf links before being broken to pieces by the force of the tide.

The railway company learnt a lesson from this watery episode and used their initiative to give passengers, liable to suffer the discomfort of further floods, new access to drier ground. They constructed a temporary raised walkway, about five feet off the ground, complete with a handrail, that served until remedial work was completed to repel the floods.

In early December 2000 Dawlish Warren made the national news when the valley in which Hazelwood caravan park is sited was flooded to a depth of several feet. The Coastguard co-ordinated an overnight rescue which saw 160 residents, cats, dogs and a parrot rowed in an Environment Agency inflatable boat, or air lifted by the Chivenor-based air-sea rescue helicopter, to dry ground. They were then taken to Dawlish Leisure Centre.

The Shutterton Brook, normally an anonymous watercourse, was just one small stream of a great many in Devon to overflow its banks during this storm. The situation arose at the end of one of the wettest autumns when the ground simply could absorb no more water. In combination with a high tide the waters of the stream, unable to disperse, were ponded back.

The same night two people were drowned at Cheriton Fitzpaine when their car was washed away by another small brook in spate.

One of the most unusual Warren homes, in the 1920s and '30s, was a small former cargo boat called *Kate*, which belonged to Mr Stear, an Exeter antique dealer. He had transformed it, over a period of many years, into a fine home complete with drinking water and even a colourful figurehead. During one storm he was so worried about her, moored in the middle of the forty-yard wide creek, that he had to go and check on her. A similar, smaller boat, moored beside the *Kate*, was carried 500 yards and dumped on the edge of the golf course. It normally took him a minute or two to take his punt the twenty or so yards that she was moored from the shore. However, attempting this at the height of the storm took him a battling two hours. In this time he was carried up the creek no less than three times! *Kate*, moored close to the Round House and held in position by six heavy anchors, managed to stay put. Once aboard, and satisfied that all was well, he was unable to catch the 9.00 a.m. train back to work in Exeter the following morning, as he could not get ashore until lunch time!

The *Kate* was leased out to visitors in this period. It was featured in the book *Unknown Devon* which was published in the 1920s: "*I once spent a month marooned upon Dawlish Warren, or, rather, on the little creek which separates the seaward ridge of sandhills from the golf links. My home was a ketch which, having been lost somewhere in the upper reaches of the estuary, had been salved and converted into a houseboat, and a very pleasant home she made. The* Kate, *for that was her unromantic name, suffered from none of the disadvantages of the frail bungalows to seaward of her. South-west gales, which bring huge rollers to batter the defences of the southernmost bungalows and occasionally to reduce one of them to matchwood, had no terrors for the* Kate, *or her crew. At the worst she would float, though that was a thing she never did during my tenancy; the* Kate *was far too staid to indulge lightly in any such prank. For the most part she rested high and dry on a sandbank, but twice a day the tide would creep up the little creek and lap at her black sides. Even then the* Kate *never budged an inch out of the perpendicular. One has to live upon a ship for a month to realize what a difference a little thing like that can make. Aboard the* Kate *it was possible to enjoy all the sensations of ocean travel without any of its disadvantages.*"

It's sad to relate that during the Second World War she was used as a target by RAF bombers practising attacks when flying down the estuary towards the out-of-bounds Warren and was destroyed, as it is paradoxically said, by 'friendly fire'.

In those days the Warren was divided by the tidal stream of Greenland Lake (visible in both pictures on page 14) into two long tongues of sand, the Inner and the Outer Warren. This inlet, which ran up to the railway line, probably derived its name from the trawlers which fished in Greenland waters mooring here when returning 'home'.

In the shallows, at low water, children could paddle or stand on islands of warm sand and gaze at darting shrimps. When the tide was in, the same inlet formed a deeper sea-lake and could only be crossed by boat although there was a crossing point, the remains of which, they say, are now submerged beneath the sand. The 'Bridge of Sighs', shown on this map extract of 1906, was a structure that spanned the mouth of this inlet, where the golf course was at its most distant point from the 'mainland'. Before the golf course was built there was a rifle range here and the 'Bridge of Sighs' enabled soldiers to cross the gulf between the dunes and the point from which they fired. There were also prize-shooting tournaments held here.

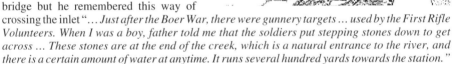

It was not always safe for those who passed by. Mr Dewdney, a local boatman, was taking a number of passengers along the coast and parallel to the Warren shore when a stray bullet impacted into the mizzen mast of his boat, just inches above his head!

In 1949 the remains of the 'Bridge of Sighs' were uncovered by the temporary conditions which prevailed at that time. It was pointed out that it was an indicator of just how much erosion had taken place at the Warren in the late 1920s, '30s and '40s.

A similar tale was told by the late Reg Colley of Starcross, a man who was greatly interested in life on the Warren. From him there was no mention of the name of the bridge but he remembered this way of crossing the inlet "... *Just after the Boer War, there were gunnery targets ... used by the First Rifle Volunteers. When I was a boy, father told me that the soldiers put stepping stones down to get across ... These stones are at the end of the creek, which is a natural entrance to the river, and there is a certain amount of water at anytime. It runs several hundred yards towards the station.*"

Greenland Lake was plugged after erosion of the Outer Warren. This was achieved by placing a railway-sleeper barrier across its mouth, allowing sands to accumulate, and then it was drained. This gully is still visible and at times it appears to be a very wet depression. The wetlands and a number of brackish ponds occupy part of this former inlet. It's possible to walk through a lower stretch of this depression which leads past the visitor centre.

My favourite book is the late Raymond B. Cattell's *Under Sail Through Red Devon*, which was first published in 1937 but republished by Obelisk Publications in two parts in 1984 and 1985. In the first part, retitled *Adventure Through Red Devon*, Ray spent a few summers, in the 1930s, on the Warren in one of those unusual bungalows. Here are a few short extracts from his timeless book, which covered the whole South Devon coastline and many of its estuaries.

"*When I think of the halcyon days that we spent on that sun-bathed wilderness of dunes, with the murmuring of ocean all around it and the endless lullaby of the wind in its sighing grasses, I am not surprised that we let spring ripen into summer and summer speed into autumn before we set out on any voyage.*

At first we thought the only vegetation was the wiry sea couch grass and the spears of marram-grass, which caught the wind-blown sand and arrested it in dunes. But soon we discovered that the island had a rare and beautiful flower life of its own. On every steep bank we found the spreading mesembryanthemum with its glaucous green leaves like a fat baby's fingers clutching here and there a star-like red or yellow flower. The pale and cloudy sea holly hid its lovely forms among sheltering dunes and the yellow-rimmed cups of spurge grew almost riotously.

We longed for a garden, but there was no earth and no water. Very well, we would create a garden. So we dug a hollow beside the house and fenced it, providing, a bastion against the wind and the marching sand dunes. Then I took Sandpiper to Littleham Cove and filled her from stem to stern with bags of rich red earth. Looking like a dangerously overloaded Thames barge, or a submerging submarine she would cross the two miles of water on calm days, quite enjoying her role as a beast of burden. The precious earth was not spread abroad but laid in wide clay gutters gently sloping from the house. The equally precious water was collected from the roof and stored in the tank from which we drew it for drinking and washing. And when it had done all for us that it could it was drained into an ingeniously arranged distributing bowl which, after aerating it, fed a little to each of the gently-sloping earth runnels.

People came from far to gaze and grin at this Heath Robinson device, but by its aid we grew lettuces, luxuriant nasturtiums, marigolds, and many other real garden flowers. Thus we made the desert blossom, but never with a rose. Thinking to give the native plants a better chance in life we transplanted them to our garden – in particular I wanted a great bush of sea holly – but one and all they pined for their desert freedom and died.

Most of the plants modified themselves amazingly to the salty conditions. The lettuces were short, stunted and very fleshy, but with a tough structure and leathery hide. This did not prevent the innumerable rabbits recognising them as a wonderful delicacy for moonlight picnics. After beating the elements we were not to be beaten by rabbits; almost every night we shot one from the window and ate it next day with green salad.

The new flowers of spring and summer did not arrive in confused order, as they do in the luxuriating Devon lanes. In this more exacting playground they came almost singly, each for a time holding sway and then fading away before the onward dance of the next. Never have I seen such definite ways of vegetation.

First the quiet colours of the spurge and holly. Then, in June, rose a silent army of tall and elegant evening primroses. Their great bells opened like large pale stars in the dusk, and when it was almost dark they positively glowed with golden light, converting the Warren to a fairy-land of Chinese lanterns wherein the moths winged their soft way to drink nectar. In high summer came the pink rest-harrow, springing from nowhere, covering everything. And then the hardy thrift and bright large periwinkle.

To a distant star, on which the passage of time is swifter than the earth, the island, with its succession of lovely hues, must have appeared like a pulsating opal. The last colour, with which autumn rang down the curtain, was the grey, ashy shade of the dying grasses.

Always the tide dominated with its inexorable rhythm the life of the Warren. Each day it swept into the estuary, changed the face of all things, held majestic sway like some monarch holding court, and departed. Woe betide the mortal who made his puny plans without consulting the movements of his majesty. The day's programme for fetching food supplies from Exmouth had to be arranged to avoid at any rate the wilder jostlings of the tidal procession. More than once I arose from my desk dismayed by the spectacle of Monica and the groceries being swept out to sea at such a speed, despite her frantic paddling, that I scarcely expected to see them again the same day." Fortunately she was none the worse for wear and, apparently, enjoyed the challenge.

Raymond B. Cattell, pictured here in 1993, went on to have a marvellous career, being an expert psychologist and author of textbooks on personality, behaviour and intelligence. Most of his working life was spent at Milwaukee but in his retirement he moved to the eternal warmth of Hawaii, where he continued to guide PhD students along their chosen paths throughout his long retirement. One of his paintings, which he proudly placed on the wall of his Hawaiian home, was of the former Warren landmark, the 'Good Ship Kate' mentioned earlier. He passed away in February 1998 at the age of 93.

Another long-term 'exile', Anthony Westell, recalled, with affection, visiting The Ship at Cockwood, a public house ran by " *'Ma Webber' a redoubtable lady who was there, at least until 1950.*" He also recalled a dinghy sailor called Joe Yorke, at the Exmouth Club, who lived at Cockwood. "*His father, Colonel Yorke, was locally famous as the man who shot a leopard when it escaped from Paignton Zoo.*"

He went on to say: "*What surprises me is that I can remember very little about the other people who had bungalows on Exmouth Warren. One I do remember, because he was my closest friend in Exeter, was John Williams. His parents were managers of the wonderful old Dellers' Café in Bedford Circus* [Exeter] *until, sometime in the 1930s, they opened the Imperial Hotel. For several years they rented a bungalow on the Warren. We were so engrossed in our world of rowing, sailing, swimming and running through the dunes that I hardly noticed other people.*

Now I think I remember how it all ended. It was in the summer of 1939. I think I can remember a policeman arriving one night, having pushed his bike across the sand dunes, to tell us to black-out our windows – we had oil lamps– because war had started ... That summer the sea was at the back wall, and the winter storms did the rest!"

All sorts of factors were cited as having been the cause of the demise of the community and colony of huts on the Outer Warren. An elderly correspondent, reflecting on his childhood days there, wrote this in *The Times*, on 1 January 1960: "*Civilization – or ruination – was creeping up on the Warren too, from the town across the river* [Exmouth]. *To increase the amenities, a long sea-drive wall was built around the bay; the tides, which had run unopposed up over the sand and sand dunes now found themselves barred by a sea wall. Inevitably, they turned on the Warren. As the years between the wars went by, the sea encroached more and more.*"

What a sad and sorry sight it must have been for the Warren home owners. After every storm houses could be seen hanging out over walls of sand whilst debris and possessions were strewn all over the beach. The north-easterly gale was the arch-enemy. If there was a winter when it made several unwelcome appearances then it was certain that acres of sand would be removed. Not much could be done to stop it. "*The frantic efforts of golf club and railway, the hurdle fences, the groins of heavy railway sleepers, would be broken like egg-shells in a night.*"

The late Eric Delderfield, author of many fine books about Devon and brother of celebrated novelist Ronnie (*To Serve Them All My Days* and *A Horseman Riding By*), wrote this in 1951 when looking back at the Warren's past: "*Since the commencement of the twentieth century, however, the sea has continually encroached on the beach and each winter since 1900 saw more of it disappear after each heavy storm. This was said to have been due in no small measure to the removal of thousands of tons of gravel from Bull Hill, the large sandbank in the river off Starcross. The gravel was used for the building of the Princess Pier, Torquay and such an outcry arose on both sides of the river that the removals were stopped. It was said that the course of the channel was being altered, but whether this was the cause of the gradual disappearance of the Warren will never be definitely known, although it is extremely likely.*"

The Warren has long been a popular place primarily for those day visitors from the Exeter area. Newspaper articles of yesteryear have made estimates of the numbers of visitors, mostly by train, that would arrive on high days and holidays when the only real attraction was the beach. On August Bank Holiday 1933, thousands flocked to the Warren. But not everyone was happy. This is part of a letter written to the *Express & Echo*, from Starcross, on 29 August:

"*Now that Dawlish Warren has become such a favourite resort ... cannot something be done to improve the sanitary arrangements on the beach and nearby?*

This summer must have witnessed record bookings to the Warren (it was estimated that there were 20,000 people there on August Bank Holiday), yet, so far as I am aware, there is not a single public convenience anywhere on the beach or nearby. The result is that the Warren is rapidly becoming a place hardly fit for human habitation.

The entrance to the beach from under the railway arch has been littered with filth for weeks, while the stench, particularly in the early morning, will, if allowed to continue, be responsible for a serious epidemic. The boulders, thrown out to protect the railway line, are now the homes of hundreds of rats, and these vermin can be seen any day nibbling at the refuse left by the holidaymakers. The litter on the beach has not been cleared once this summer, yet ice cream, fruit, chocolate and refreshment vendors do their business on this very refuse heap close to the railway arch. Flies there are – by the hundred." The 'rate payer' who had penned this letter had contacted various bodies but nobody had been prepared to accept responsibility, so the press was his 'last resort'. Prior to the First World War, a labourer, with a horse and cart, was employed one day a week to collect and remove any rubbish found along the beach.

Visitors of the past often came by railway. 'The Bathing Train' or 'The Woolworth Train' was a much-loved institution. For a modest fare of sixpence (2½p), the price of many items at Woolworths' stores, it enabled people to have a bracing early morning dip, leaving Exeter at the unearthly hour of 7.00 a.m., and an early return home.

This picture was taken in 1939 by Mr R. W. J. Norton of Larch Road, Exeter, a man who loved Devon, particularly Dartmoor. He has captured a healthy crop of farm labourers at Dawlish Warren forking up a cart-full of seaweed to be used as a manure on farms in the 'Vale of Dawlish'. The wagon which was used to transport the seaweed had balloon tyres, ideal in such soft sandy situations because it didn't get sucked down into the 'primeval ooze'.

This area, in the lee of the Haldon Hills, once famous for its fields of Devon Violets, is a most productive corner of the county. It has an excellent climate and fertile red soils made even more fruitful after the Warren weed had been added. Today on one side of the road between Starcross and Dawlish, it's the produce of the soil which dominates the land use, whilst on the other it's a case of 'grockle farming', visitors filling the fields full of tents and caravans. We jokingly call this 'in-tents-ive farming'.

During the Second World War the Warren took on a new but necessarily ugly appearance. In defence of the realm the Warren saw the arrival of gun emplacements, landmines and miles of barbed wire. Anti-aircraft guns, searchlights and other installations were also placed to offer, at the very least, some determined resistance to any potential attacks. The beach was put out-of-bounds by the War Office, an unavoidable state of affairs that was to last well beyond the end of the war.

Several locals were evacuated from their homes, to the west of the railway line, in order that troops could be billeted. The railway line sometimes came under aerial attack.

The main difference between the pre-war and post-war Warren was that there was a lot less of it to roam, a series of war-time storms having stripped it of most of its sand. The colony of Bohemian-styled bungalows at the distal end of the sandspit had virtually been washed away; that is, apart from a couple of battered shanties and two concrete water tanks which were left standing.

In January 1946 a south-westerly gale accounted for the last few of the besieged Outer Warren bungalows. After three more years late autumn storms removed large volumes of sand and it was recorded that much of the ninth tee of the Warren's golf course had suffered the same ignominious fate.

The last of the permanent Warren 'houses' to go was one whose address was White Shanty, Ninth Green, Dawlish Warren. This was the rented home, from 1946 to 1960, of Basil and Peggy Macer-Wright. A condition of their lease dictated that they had to vacate each August as the owners used it as a summer home. This was not a problem because they simply swapped homes with their landlords.

In late September 1960 a combination of high tides and a south-easterly gale removed the dunes on which their home was built. They salvaged what they could and their bath was duly dug out of the sand and placed on the ninth green! White Shanty, although now just a memory, can justly stake the claim of being the last 'permanent' home ever to stand on this part of the Warren, thereby marking the end of an era of duneland habitation.

Dawlish Warren had already long been written off by some. In a lecture delivered to the boys of Exeter's Ladysmith Secondary Modern Boys' School in April 1950, Mr C. Kidson, lecturer in Geography at the University College of the South West and a leading expert in marine matters, told them that this sandspit was doomed to disappear within ten years. Using lantern slides he highlighted the plight of the former 'Warren-end village' that once boasted about 70 bungalows and a store. He told the boys that the two bungalows that survived had no future, as all that would be left of the Warren would be just a rash of numerous small sandy islands. He also insisted that the railway line would have to be re-routed further inland and delivered this further thought: *"The solution is to build a sea wall right across the front, but the expense involved would be too heavy and the result would probably not be worth the money!"*

Fortunately, despite Mr Kidson's prediction of doom, the Warren was still there for the following decades and the railway still brought huge numbers of day visitors. On August Bank Holiday Monday in 1955 some 6,800 people arrived by train, many more than ever went on to the more established resorts of Dawlish or Teignmouth. The crowd was swollen to more than 20,000 by day-trippers driving to the Warren and by those holidaying in the district.

For those who stayed longer there were some unusual forms of holiday home. Camping Coaches, in the shape of railway carriages, were placed in sidings near the station. Here people can still stay in carriages with such proud names as Exeter, Plymouth, Gloucester and so on. The GWR established similar Camping Coaches at a number of stations in Devon including Lustleigh, and at Ide, Chudleigh and Ashton on the former Teign Valley branch line.

It is most likely that regular Warren devotees of the past would have possessed a beach hut. Shangri-La, Beggar's Roost, Sandpiper, Dunroamin' and so on, complete with 'home comforts', formed quite a colony of multi-coloured retreats, 'bolt-holes' from the fun of the nearby beach. When they were about to meet their demise, not through the tempest of wind and wave but by 'officialdom', there were 432 of them. They had stalwartly served as safe havens to see out an occasional sharp downpour or provide a shaded sanctuary from the searing heat of the noon-day

sun. This picture was taken at that sad time when it was decreed that they would have to go. Those who didn't dismantle and transport them away left them to be burnt. With them must have gone a mountain of memories of fun-filled days at the beach. For many it was the end of an era; the new, uniform, sterile-looking huts not for them. These replacements were no greater adornment to the

Warren than their forerunners and, unlike Dr Who's Tardis, were no bigger inside than they looked from without and nowhere near as popular.

The Warren's 'protectors' have appeared in various guises. They include engineers whose concrete revetments, rock armour, groynes, gabions, wave baffles and so on have helped to keep

the sandspit intact. There is an army of caring conservationists who have created ponds, built board walks, buried old Christmas trees in order to stabilise the dunes ('dune thatching'), erected brush-wood barriers and lavished a lot of tender loving care and attention on this magical place.

There have been arguments about how best to prevent the sea damaging or destroying this sandspit. Those who have diligently studied the Warren's changing faces have looked at most of the possible or probable reasons for the changes in its shape and size. They have considered the effect of the apparent straightening of the coastline by Man's building of the railway along the

estuary and coast in the 1840s and also the building of an extended esplanade at Exmouth. They have studied the prevailing winds and the type and nature of the beach materials found there; they have even looked at the rainfall pattern in determining the flow of water down the river Exe. They have examined the impact of visitors en masse and 'taken on board' several other factors. The various debates about Dawlish Warren have occupied enough local newspaper column space to have reached the distal end of the Warren, many times.

The stormy winter of 1990, when the western, landward end of the Warren was under threat, was yet another episode in a long-running battle between it and the sea. The supply of beach materials, needed to keep the natural balance between the effects of the forces of erosion and those of deposition, had been greatly reduced following the construction of the unbroken sea wall built to protect the main-line rail route. Although it's a more complicated story than just this it became imperative to take further action to protect the Warren. In the months between February and September 1992 the scene was

one of intense activity and people came to marvel at the machines and the methods employed. It was not just a case of placing heavy objects in the way of the storm in the hope that they would

repel the maritime threat. The scientifically designed scheme had many objectives. The wave energy had to be dissipated, and the base of the structure had to be such that it could withstand the constant, relentless undercutting of the sea. For many reasons, all of them practical, Larvikite was brought all the way from Norway! As the project neared completion it was realised that not enough rock had been imported, so limestone from the Mendip Hills in Somerset was used to finish the scheme.

And despite all the upheaval of the extensive beach works the birds of passage continued to arrive and feed in the Warren's richly resourced 'back garden', the Exe Estuary. Up to 8,000 birds in winter and over 600 species of plants have been recorded here. This 505-acre site was awarded the status of National Nature Reserve on 15 June 2000.

For those who wish to share this love of wildlife the warden service arrange a number of guided walks throughout each season. The delights of plants like the Warren Crocus (*Romutea columnae*), which flowers from April to June, are there to be discovered. This is the only place in mainland Britain where it is found.

The Visitor Centre and its staff have done much excellent work in educating students about the Warren environment and its ecology. Inside there are a large marine aquarium and a life-sized model made of 'rubbish' collected from the Warren – a reminder for people not to drop or leave rubbish behind.

The Warren's sandy shore was dubbed 'the Killer Beach' in the 1930s when inquest followed inquest as many bathers met a watery end. In July 1935 a young couple were washed to their deaths whilst four others who tried to rescue them were saved after a frantic struggle with a stormy sea. A month later, in August 1935, an Exeter man lost his life in trying to save a thirteen-year-old who had been swept out to sea whilst seven more, who had got into difficulties, had to be pulled out of the water. The lessons were not learned; five days later a Londoner was drowned at the Warren. This ultimately resulted in recommendations to rectify the dangerous situation. But

talk is cheap and three decades elapsed before the Dawlish Warren Life Saving Club was formed in June 1966, this following a meeting of concerned councillors, police and other bodies. Since those pre-Baywatch days this stalwart Club has overseen the beach with a professional eye. Its members have rescued many people, sometimes in very dangerous circumstances, so their presence is a reassuring one to the thousands who gather here when the weather is set fair in high summer.

To keep them in peak condition they participate in various life-saving competetions, taking on similar groups from across the nation and throughout the world with a degree of success.

One of the best views over Dawlish Warren is to be had from the Mount Pleasant Inn that sits atop a low cliff. As these two photos show, the inn has changed considerably in appearance over the years. This appeared in the local press in January 1938: *"Few of Dominic Stone's many friends would recognise the attractive house in our photograph as the old Mount Pleasant Inn at Dawlish Warren. The ever-popular holiday house of call, with its magnificent views of the estuary, golf course and sea, has now been completely remodelled by its owners, the Heavitree Brewery Limited of Exeter, who, while providing greatly increased accommodation and modern comforts, have been careful to preserve the old-fashioned character of the house. Mr Kemys-Jenkin, FRIBA, the architect, and Mr Mallett, the Dawlish builder, are to be congratulated on their success."*

In the middle of August 1955 the Mount Pleasant Inn caught fire. Attempts to put out the blaze were thwarted by the lack of water pressure in the mains, so it called for drastic measures. Hurriedly a chain of about 200 volunteer holidaymakers formed to help salvage whatever items could be saved. Fire engines raced to the scene from Newton Abbot, Dawlish and Teignmouth and within 90 minutes the fire was brought under control. The guests were found alternative accommodation at various houses in the district.

The Mount Pleasant Inn once possessed a highly active poltergeist guilty of removing jars from

a shelf and throwing them around. One former employee, and a number of guests, looked on in astonishment as a bunch of keys lifted off a hook and crashed onto the floor many yards away.

Close by is the Langstone Cliff Hotel. Built in the late eighteenth century, it was once the grand home of Mr Avant Washington, after whom the hotel's ballroom suite is named. The hotel's story is one of success. Stanley and Marjorie Rogers kept a fish and chip shop in Exeter until 1946. With an eye to getting a bargain, Stanley visited Dawlish to attend a furniture auction only to find that it was the property which was being auctioned, the furniture having been scheduled for the next day. You can imagine his wife's surprise when he returned home to announce that he had bought a 'hotel'!

The couple returned the next day intending to purchase as many of the fittings and furniture as they could afford. It had been a beautiful home and there would have been many bargains but unfortunately a golden opportunity was missed as Stanley's mother, who accompanied them, tripped on entering the front door and ended up in hospital with a broken arm. The new owners missed the auction!

After the harsh winter of 1947 the modestly sized 12-bedroomed hotel opened its doors on 30 March. Stanley and Marjorie both passed away in 1970 but the Rogers family continued to run it and in 1997 celebrated the fiftieth anniversary of the family's association with it. Since its humble beginnings, it has grown in status, size and style and has entertained many famous guests.

This landward side of the railway line has been developed since the Second World War. The earliest camps, started about 1951/52, included the Welcome Stranger and Hazelwood. Some further inland have also become popular. The drive between Cockwood and Dawlish, along the A379, takes the motorist past Cofton Country and Lady's Mile, to name but two, both having made much progress in the facilities they offer.

Locals are often heard to say that they 'prefer the Warren in winter', when the hordes of holidaymakers have gone, when the car parks are cheaper, and when it's a truly wild and wondrous place, a wave-washed wilderness.

Our look at the Warren has almost run its course but we shouldn't leave it without letting the late, great Raymond B. Cattell tell us about how he remembered the last of his memorable days here in the mid-1930s.

"There is always something melancholy, as of an empty ballroom when the lamps expire, about this fair county when the throngs of visitors depart. Then the faithful, who will stay with her in winter as in summer, prepare themselves to enjoy space and solitude – but the moment of change is melancholy.

Yet summer lingers on, mellow and serene, until one begins to believe it will never go. In the middle of October one may still bathe and sunbathe, or sail over calm seas to picnic in uninhabited coves, draped with trees still heavy with unfaded summer green.

Winter becomes a tale told long ago. But a day dawns with leaden clouds to the east; the late equinoctial gales have begun. A storm, bracing everyone for winter, bursts upon all the coasts. There is little rain but much scudding cloud wrack. Ships huddle in the bay like frightened sheep whilst the beaches are ruthlessly washed clear of summer debris. Even tents, deck chairs and pier furniture go floating off to sea.

So it happened that year at the Warren. Summer seemed still in entire possession when the time came for us to go. By the light of a sadly reproachful late harvest moon, we ferried away our last belongings ... but we left even as winter came; for next morning the grey, threatening sea, lashed into foam by the east wind, was already beginning to overrun the Warren."

Perhaps we don't have to understand the Warren's geography, or know of its history, to enjoy a bracing walk along it. But maybe a little knowledge will help us come to understand and care why we really shouldn't take this extremely delicate environment for granted. Hopefully this book will help to put 'The Story of Dawlish Warren' into some sort of sandy perspective ...